AI FOR BUSINESS MASTERY:

UNLOCKING THE FUTURE WITH

SMART TECH

Transforming Industries and Innovations with Artificial Intelligence

AUTHOR: HUATENG OU

A freelance writer currently residing in the prairie province of Canada.

Author of several medium-to-long-length novels, with forward-looking articles on AI published on various platforms in both Chinese and English.

Possessing a profound research background and unique insights into the field of artificial intelligence, dedicated to exploring the future directions of AI development.

The expansive landscapes and cultural environment of the prairie province provide endless creative inspiration.

FOREWORD

In the 21st century, artificial intelligence (AI) has become an indispensable part of our lives and work. From intelligent smartphone assistants to self-driving cars, AI technology is profoundly altering our

2

lifestyles and work patterns. However, the development of AI has not been an overnight success; it has gone through decades of ups and downs before gradually entering the public's consciousness.

A Brief Overview of the Development of AI Technology

- From the early days of symbolic reasoning to the evolution of modern deep learning: In the 1950s, symbolic reasoning dominated AI research, with researchers attempting to simulate human thinking through symbolic logic. However, with the advancement of computer technology, machine learning and deep learning gradually became the core of AI research.

- Milestones and Key Technologies in AI: The perceptron, an early neural network model, laid the foundation for later deep learning. Expert systems reached their peak in the 1980s, capable of simulating expert decision-making processes. Subsequently, the emergence of machine learning and deep learning technologies ushered in a new era of AI research.

- Current Status and Data of AI Technology Applications: The global AI market is experiencing unprecedented growth, projected to reach billions of dollars in the coming years, according to the latest data. Particularly in China and the United States, AI technology has seen widespread application and investment.

- Primary Directions of Investment and Research in AI within Industries: Natural language processing and computer vision are the current focal points of AI research. From chatbots to image recognition, these technologies are bringing revolutionary changes to our lives.
- How AI is Reshaping Business and Life: Use cases of AI in daily life include smart home devices like intelligent speakers and light bulbs, which have become commonplace. Autonomous driving technology is also gradually maturing, with a significant number of self-driving cars expected to hit the roads in the near future.
- Impact of AI on Traditional Industry Transformation: In the medical field, AI technology is aiding doctors in disease diagnosis and treatment. In manufacturing, intelligent robots are replacing traditional production lines, thereby enhancing production efficiency.

AI technology is profoundly altering the way we live and work. As a reader, you will delve into the developmental journey of AI, its current application landscape, and how it is reshaping both business and daily life within this book. It is our hope that this book will provide you with valuable insights and inspiration.

TABLE OF CONTENTS

CHAPTER 1 AI ASSISTS CONTENT CREATION

Text content: ChatGPT and other AI writing tool applications

Developmental Journey and Applications of AI Natural Language Generation Technology

Early-stage Applications: In the initial phases of NLG, rule-based and template-driven systems were employed to generate fixed-format reports such as weather forecasts and stock market updates.

Application of Statistical Models: With the advancement of statistical learning methods, NLG started being used to generate more natural customer service responses, email summaries, and the like.

Utilization of Deep Learning: Through the use of RNNs and LSTMs, businesses gained the ability to generate more complex texts, including marketing advertisements and personalized news summaries.

Application of Transformer Architecture: Leveraging models like BERT and the GPT series, both enterprises and creators have the capability to generate high-quality articles, short texts, poems, and even novels.

The technical principles, advantages and specific applications of ChatGPT:

content creation

Blogs and Articles: Generate initial drafts using ChatGPT, followed by human editing for refinement and enhancement.

Advertisement Copy: Craft tailored ad copy for diverse target audiences.

Storytelling: Provide writers with suggestions and inspiration for story plots.

customer service robot

Instant Replies: Integrate ChatGPT into websites or applications to provide users with 24/7 instant replies.

Automatic FAQ Generation: Automatically generate FAQ pages based on common user questions.

programming assistant

Code Suggestions: Offer developers suggestions for code snippets.

Error Detection: Automatically detect errors in code and provide suggestions for fixes.

Specific Applications of AI in News Writing and Information Production:

Automated News Generation

Real-time Reporting: For rapidly evolving events such as sports games and stock market fluctuations, utilize AI to swiftly produce preliminary reports. Data-Driven Reporting: Automatically analyze vast amounts of data to generate reports about weather, traffic, and market trends.

Personalized Information Recommendations

User Profile Construction: Analyze users' browsing history and preferences to construct user profiles.

Content Recommendations: Based on user profiles, provide recommendations for information they might find interesting.

Content Review and Optimization

Automatic Summarization: Generate summaries for lengthy articles, offering readers a quick overview.

Keyword Optimization: Analyze article content to add or optimize keywords, enhancing search engine rankings.

Case Study: How to Use ChatGPT for Content Creation

Registration and Login:

Visit the official OpenAI website to register. https://openai.com/

Log in to your account and access the ChatGPT interface.

Model Selection:

OpenAI offers various versions of GPT models, such as GPT-2, GPT-3, etc. Choose the appropriate model version.

Enter Prompts:

In the input box, provide prompts for the content you want the AI to generate. For example, "Write an article about the application of AI in the medical field."

Generate Content:

14

Click the "Generate" button and wait for the AI to produce content for you.

The generated content will appear in the output box.

Edit and Refine:

Edit and refine the content generated by the AI as needed.

You can input different prompts multiple times to get more content suggestions.

```
+-------------------------------------+
|                    |                |
| User: Hi CHATgpt, how are you?      |
|                    |                |
| CHATgpt: Hello! I'm just a program, |
| so I don't have feelings, but I'm   |
| ready to assist you.            |
|                    |                |
+-------------------------------------+
```

Case: How to use AI tools to automatically generate news reports

Selecting the Right AI News Generation Tool:

Choose an appropriate AI news generation tool based on your needs, such as Wordsmith by Automated Insights.

Data Input:

Input the data you want to report, such as scores from sports events or stock market fluctuations, into the tool.

Template Selection and Configuration:

Select an appropriate news reporting template or customize one according to your requirements.

Configure parameters like reporting style and length.

Generating the Report:

Click the "Generate" button and wait for the tool to create the news report for you.

Edit and refine the generated report as necessary.

Guide to Using Wordsmith by Automated Insights:

Wordsmith is an automated content generation platform developed by Automated Insights. It can automatically generate textual content based on data, such as news reports and financial statements. Below is a guide on how to use Wordsmith:

1.Registration and Login:

- Visit the official website of Automated Insights.
- Choose the Wordsmith product and proceed with registration.
- Log in using your registered account information.

2. Create a New Project:

- On the Dashboard, click the "Create New Project" button.
- Name the project and choose an appropriate template or create a new one.

3. Data Input:

- Wordsmith supports various data input methods, including direct input, CSV file upload, or API integration.
- Select the suitable data input method and import the data into the project.

4. Set Rules and Templates:

- In the template editor, establish rules for the data. For instance, if stock prices rise, set up text to generate like "Stock prices are up."
- Use double curly braces {{ }} to insert data fields, such as {{stock_price}}.
- Add conditional statements like IF, ELSE, etc., as needed to create diverse text content.

5. Generate Text Content:

- In the template editor, click the "Preview" button to view the generated text content.
- If satisfied, save the template and commence content generation.

6.Publish and Share:

- Generated text content can be directly published on the Wordsmith platform or exported in formats like CSV, TXT, etc.
- The generated content can also be published directly to other platforms or applications using APIs.

7. Analysis and Optimization:

- Wordsmith provides content analysis tools to assess content generation effectiveness and audience reactions.

18

- Based on analysis results, optimize templates and rules to enhance content quality and effectiveness.

Image Content: Applications of AI Drawing Tools like DALL-E

1. Advancements from Image Recognition to Image Generation Technology:

Image Recognition: Early AI image technologies primarily focused on image recognition, utilizing techniques like Convolutional Neural Networks (CNN) for tasks such as image classification and object detection. Tools like TensorFlow and Caffe provided open-source frameworks that made it easy for developers to construct and train image recognition models.

How to Use TensorFlow for Image Recognition:

- Install the TensorFlow library.
- Utilize pretrained models or train your own from scratch.
- Input image data, perform predictions, and classifications.

Image Generation: With the emergence of Generative Adversarial Networks (GANs), image generation technology has made significant strides. GANs can produce high-quality, realistic images. Tools like DALL-E and StyleGAN are image generation tools built upon GANs.

2. Innovations and Future Applications of DALL-E:

DALL-E: An image generation model launched by OpenAI, capable of generating images based on textual descriptions.

Innovations:

- High-Quality Image Generation: DALL-E produces images with high resolution and realism.
- Diversity: For the same textual description, DALL-E can generate images with varying styles and content.
- Detail Handling: DALL-E captures details from textual descriptions accurately in the generated images.

Future Applications:

- Artistic Creation: Artists can use DALL-E to create unique artworks.
- Advertising Design: Advertising companies can rapidly generate ad sketches or concept visuals using DALL-E.

20

- Game Development: Game developers can utilize DALL-E to generate characters, scenes, and other elements in games.

How to Use DALL-E:

- Visit the official OpenAI website and access the DALL-E interface.
- Input a textual description, such as "a cat wearing a spacesuit," in the input box.
- Click the "Generate" button and wait for DALL-E to create an image for you.
- View the generated image and download or share it as needed.

Applications and Tips for Using DALL-E:

Applications:

Custom Artwork: An artist used DALL-E to generate a series of customized artworks based on client descriptions, such as an image depicting "stars and moons dancing in the solar system."

Educational Aid: A school employed DALL-E to generate images related to course content, assisting students in better understanding and remembering knowledge.

Product Design: A furniture company utilized DALL-E to create a range of "future-style" furniture design concepts, inspiring product development.

Usage Tips:

1. Clear Descriptions: The results from DALL-E largely depend on the input text description. To achieve satisfactory outcomes, it's recommended to provide clear and specific descriptions.

2. Multiple Attempts: For the same text description, DALL-E might generate images with different styles and content. If unsatisfied with the initial result, trying multiple times is advisable until a desired image is obtained.

3. Combine with Other Tools: Generated images from DALL-E can be combined with other image editing tools like Photoshop for further optimization and refinement.

4. Copyright Considerations: While images generated by DALL-E are original, copyright issues still need attention, particularly for commercial use, to ensure no infringement of others' rights.

MidJourney and Other AI Drawing Tools

MidJourney is an AI-powered drawing software that operates through Discord's AI drawing tools. Users can generate images by interacting with the MidJourney Bot using text. It utilizes deep learning algorithms to assist users in their artistic creations. Through learning from a large dataset of artwork, MidJourney understands various drawing styles and techniques, enabling users to easily create personalized pieces. This software is applicable in various drawing domains, including illustration, comics, and oil painting. Both professional artists and enthusiasts can find suitable creative methods within MidJourney.

Methods of Image Generation

MidJourney offers three main methods of image generation:

- Text-to-Image: Users can describe key elements of an image scene in the input box, and the AI will generate a corresponding artwork based on the description.
- Image-to-Image: Users can upload an image of a specific style and describe the image's key aspects. The AI will then generate a new image with the same style.
- Blend-to-Image: Users can input multiple images to the AI for blending, resulting in a new artwork that combines elements from various images.

Using Midjourney on Discord:

Servers and Channels:

Midjourney has a dedicated server on Discord, offering channels for collaboration, technical and billing support, official announcements, feedback, and discussions.

Users can view all joined chat rooms in the server list.

Users can also create their own servers and collaborate one-on-one with the Midjourney Bot, avoiding interference from other users' information.

Generating Images:

Users can enter the /imagine command in any #newbies channel and generate images based on prompts.

Generated images appear in a grid at low resolution. Users can choose an image from the grid for further actions, such as zooming, redoing, or creating variations.

Image Manipulation:

U1 U2 U3 U4 U buttons: Zoom in on an image, generating a larger version with more detail.

Redo button: Rerun the operation, generating a new grid of images.

24

V1 V2 V3 V4 V buttons: Create incremental variations of the selected grid image.

Additional Features:

- Users can participate in fun themed activities in the #daily-theme channel.
- Using the /daily_theme command, users can turn off notifications for that channel.
- Users can also interact with image tasks using various emojis, such as sending images via direct message, cancelling ongoing tasks, or deleting images.
- Midjourney provides users with a user-friendly AI drawing platform. With simple text interactions on Discord, users can generate artwork with personalized styles.

Leonardo:

Introduction:

Leonardo is an integrated solution introduced by SAP, encompassing various AI and machine learning tools, such as image recognition, natural language processing, predictive analysis, and more. Leonardo aims to assist businesses in harnessing data effectively, enhancing operational efficiency, and fostering innovation capabilities.

Usage Guidelines:

1. Registration and Login: Visit the official SAP Leonardo website for registration and login.
2. Select Tools: On the Leonardo dashboard, choose the desired tools, such as "Image Recognition."
3. Upload Data: Click the "Upload" button to select the images or data files you want to analyze.
4. Configure Parameters: Adjust tool parameters as needed, such as recognition accuracy, model type, etc.
5. Run Analysis: Click the "Run" button and await completion of the analysis process.
6. View Results: Once analysis is finished, review the result report, including image labels, prediction outcomes, analytical charts, and more.
7. Save and Share: You can save analysis results as report files or share them with team members.

Audio Content: Applications of AI Voice Synthesis, Music Composition, and More

Development History of AI Voice Synthesis Technology

Early Stages: The initial stages of voice synthesis technology relied primarily on rule-based approaches, generating speech through predefined speech segments and rules. The results from this method often sounded unnatural and robotic.

Statistical Models: As technology advanced, researchers began utilizing statistical models such as Hidden Markov Models (HMMs) to generate more natural speech. This approach involved predicting speech features through learning from a substantial amount of speech data.

Rise of Deep Learning: In recent years, deep learning techniques, especially Recurrent Neural Networks (RNNs) and Long Short-Term Memory Networks (LSTMs), have seen significant success in the field of voice synthesis. Examples include Google's WaveNet and OpenAI's

GPT-3, both utilizing deep learning techniques to produce high-quality speech.

The Potential and Challenges of AI in Music Composition

Potential:

Automated Composition: AI can automatically generate music based on given styles or emotions.

Music Style Transfer: AI can transform a song from one style to another, such as converting classical music to jazz.

Personalized Music Recommendations: Based on user listening history and preferences, AI can recommend or generate personalized music.

Challenges:

Creativity and Emotion: While AI can create music, it lacks genuine creativity and emotion. Music is not just notes and melodies; it also carries the composer's emotions and stories.

Copyright Issues: When AI-generated music resembles existing compositions, it may lead to copyright disputes.

Technical Limitations: Despite significant advancements in AI music composition, there are still limitations. For instance, generating lengthy high-quality music remains a challenge.

28

Cases of AI Music Composition:

1. AIVA (Artificial Intelligence Virtual Artist)

Introduction: AIVA is an AI music composition tool trained on a vast collection of classical music pieces. It can automatically generate music for instruments like piano and orchestral compositions.

Applications: AIVA has been utilized in various projects, including film scoring and background music for advertisements. It even holds the distinction of being recognized as the world's first AI composer. In 2019, it composed a symphony for the Luxembourg Philharmonic Orchestra.

2. Jukebox by OpenAI

Introduction: Jukebox, developed by OpenAI, is an AI music generation tool capable of creating music in a variety of genres, including rock, pop, and jazz.

Applications: Jukebox has produced thousands of songs, which have been released on its official website. These songs encompass not only melodies but also lyrics and vocals.

User Experience of AI Speech Synthesis:

1. Google Duplex

Introduction: Google Duplex is an AI assistant that can mimic human voice to make phone appointments or inquiries.

User Experience: Many users have noted that conversing with Google Duplex feels just like talking to a real person. Its voice sounds incredibly natural and it can understand and respond to complex questions.

2. Descript's Overdub

Introduction: Overdub is a speech synthesis tool introduced by Descript. It generates speech based on user voice samples.

Applications: Many podcasters and video creators use Overdub to edit or replace their recordings, saving time and increasing efficiency. User feedback indicates that the speech generated by Overdub is almost indistinguishable from a human voice.

AI holds significant potential in audio content creation, particularly in music and speech synthesis. However, it also faces certain technical and ethical challenges. With advancements in technology, we can anticipate even greater breakthroughs in the fields of music and speech synthesis through AI.

Video Content: Applications of AI Automated Editing, Actor Replacement, and Video Generation Tools

1. AI Automated Editing:

Introduction: AI automated editing refers to the use of AI technology to automatically select, edit, and combine video clips to create a coherent video story.

Applications: For instance, IBM's Watson AI was used to create a trailer for the 20th Century Fox film "Morgan." Watson analyzed hours of raw footage and then automatically selected the best segments for editing.

2. Actor Replacement and Deepfake Technology:

Principle: Deepfake technology employs deep learning algorithms, particularly Generative Adversarial Networks (GANs), to create realistic fake videos. This technique can replace faces in videos, making one person appear to be another.

Future Applications: While deepfake technology holds significant potential in film effects, advertising, and entertainment, it has also raised ethical and security concerns as it can be used to generate fake news or misleading information.

3.How AI Enhances Efficiency for Video Producers:

Video Editing: AI can automatically identify and label key frames, scenes, and objects in videos, speeding up the editing process.

Color Correction: AI can automatically analyze and adjust the color balance of videos, making them look more natural and professional.

Sound Enhancement: AI can automatically identify and remove background noise, enhancing audio quality.

4. Case Study: How Short Video Platforms Utilize AI:

TikTok: TikTok uses AI algorithms to recommend videos that users might enjoy. The algorithm analyzes user interactions, watch time, and preferences to suggest similar content.

Kuaishou: Kuaishou employs AI technology to automatically identify and label content within videos, such as dances, singing, and cooking, making it easier for users to discover and search for content.

Video Content: Applications of AI in Video Production

1. Practical Applications of AI Automated Editing:

Reebok Advertisement: Reebok used AI technology to analyze its past advertisements, identified audience-favored elements, and automatically created a new ad using these elements. This not only saved time but also ensured consistency between the ad and the brand.

2.Practical Applications of Deepfake Technology:

"Star Wars: The Rise of Skywalker": In this film, the late actress Carrie Fisher's face was "revived" and integrated into new scenes using deepfake technology.

3.Experience Sharing of AI in Video Editing:

Automated Trimming: Many YouTubers and short video creators use AI tools to automatically trim their videos. These tools can recognize and remove lengthy or repetitive segments, speeding up the editing process.

Audio Sync: For creators who need to synchronize audio and video in post-production, AI tools can automatically identify lip movement and sound, ensuring perfect synchronization.

4. AI Application Experience on Short Video Platforms:

Personalized Recommendations: Many short video creators find that by analyzing AI-recommended data, they can better understand audience preferences and create more popular content.

AI Filters and Effects: Many short video creators use AI tools to add filters and effects, such as background blurring, facial enhancements, and animated elements. These tools can automatically recognize objects and scenes in the video and apply effects accordingly.

AI technology is fundamentally changing the way video production and distribution are approached. From automated editing to deep fakes,

AI provides powerful tools for video producers to enhance efficiency,

create higher-quality content, and better engage with their audience.

Revolutionary Applications of AI in Video and Audio Content Creation

With the continuous advancement of technology, AI has penetrated

various aspects of our daily lives, especially in the realm of content

creation. In this chapter, we delve deep into how AI is revolutionizing

the creation of video and audio content.

Firstly, we explore how AI leverages automated editing techniques

to provide efficient and innovative solutions for advertising and film

production. These technologies not only save significant amounts of

time but also ensure high-quality content that aligns with brand

consistency.

Next, the emergence of deepfake technology, despite posing ethical and security challenges, exhibits its immense potential in applications within the film and entertainment industries. For instance, its usage in "Star Wars" to "resurrect" deceased actors showcases its significant possibilities.

In the domain of audio, AI's applications are equally noteworthy. From automatic music composition to sound optimization, AI empowers musicians and podcasters with potent tools, making it easier for them to create high-quality pieces.

On short video platforms, AI applications like personalized recommendations and automatic effects additions offer creators more opportunities to engage with their audience, simultaneously providing viewers with richer and more personalized content.

AI technology has opened up an entirely new world for content creators, offering limitless possibilities. Whether it's video, music, or other forms of content, AI provides us with more efficient and innovative ways to create and share. We can anticipate that in the future, AI will continue to lead the development of the content creation field, bringing us even more exciting innovations.

CHAPTER 2: AI-DRIVEN E-COMMERCE

With the rapid development of e-commerce, the application of AI technology in it is also increasing, bringing unprecedented convenience to merchants and consumers.

AI product recommendation technology and application

Introduction: AI product recommendation technology is a core functionality in e-commerce websites and applications. It can recommend relevant products to users based on their behavior, preferences, and historical data.

Applications: Virtually all major e-commerce platforms, such as Amazon, Taobao, and JD.com, employ AI technology to offer personalized product recommendations, thereby enhancing conversion rates and user satisfaction.

Fundamental Principles and Techniques of Recommendation Algorithms

Collaborative Filtering: This is one of the most commonly utilized recommendation algorithms, which predicts products users might like based on their past behaviors. For instance, if both User A and User B favor products X and Y, then when User A expresses interest in product Z, the system would recommend product Z to User B.

Deep Learning: In recent years, the application of deep learning technology in recommendation systems has become increasingly widespread. By training intricate neural network models, the system can more accurately predict user preferences.

Implementation of Personalized Recommendations and Its Application in E-commerce

User Profiles: By analyzing users' search history, purchase records, and browsing behavior, e-commerce platforms can create detailed user profiles for each individual. This enables the provision of more personalized recommendations.

Case Study

Amazon: Amazon is a pioneer in AI recommendation technology. Its "Recommended for You" feature offers highly personalized product recommendations to users, making it a cornerstone of Amazon's competitive advantage.

AI technology is fundamentally transforming the landscape of e-commerce, providing both merchants and consumers with a more intelligent and personalized shopping experience. As technology continues to advance, we can expect AI's applications in the e-commerce sector to become even broader and more profound.

AI User Profile Building Technology and Precision Targeting

In the realms of e-commerce and digital marketing, understanding and comprehending users is crucial. By constructing user profiles and employing AI technology for precise targeting, businesses can effectively engage with their target audience, ultimately boosting conversion rates and customer satisfaction.

Definition and Methods of User Profile Building

Definition: User profiles, also known as customer personas or buyer personas, are virtual data-based user models that describe the characteristics, behaviors, and needs of a typical user.

Methods of Building

40

Data Collection: Gather user data from various sources such as website browsing history, purchase records, social media interactions, and more.

Feature Extraction: Identify which features are key to describing users, such as age, gender, geographical location, interests, etc.

Segmentation and Classification: Group users into different segments or niche markets based on distinct features and behaviors.

AI User Profile Building Technology and Precise Targeting

In the realms of e-commerce and digital marketing, understanding and comprehending how to utilize AI technology for user behavior analysis and prediction is crucial.

Behavior Analysis: AI algorithms can automatically analyze vast amounts of user data, identifying patterns and trends to provide in-depth insights into user behavior.

Predictive Models: Utilizing machine learning techniques such as regression analysis, decision trees, and neural networks, predict users' future behaviors, such as purchase intent and churn rates.

Strategies and Implementation for Precise Targeting

Personalized Content: Based on user profiles and behavior analysis, offer personalized content and recommendations to each user, such as specific product suggestions and customized news summaries.

Multi-channel Delivery: Utilize various channels such as email, social media, mobile apps, etc., for precise targeting to ensure that information reaches the intended audience.

Real-time Interaction: Utilize AI technology for real-time analysis, adjusting and optimizing targeting strategies based on users' real-time behavior. For instance, when a user browses a specific product, provide immediate relevant offers or promotional information.

By constructing user profiles and employing AI technology for precise targeting, businesses can gain a deeper understanding of their users, enabling them to provide more personalized and tailored content and services. This not only enhances user satisfaction but also boosts conversion rates and increases sales revenue.

AI Bidirectional Advertising Placement Technology and Performance Optimization

In the realm of digital advertising, the application of AI technology is transforming the ways of purchasing, delivering, and optimizing ads. Through AI-driven bidirectional ad placement, advertisers can precisely target their desired audience while simultaneously enhancing ad effectiveness and return on investment (ROI).

Programmatic Purchasing and the Mechanism of AI Bidirectional Advertising

Programmatic Purchasing: This is an automated process of buying ads, enabling advertisers to purchase and place ads in real-time. This approach utilizes data and algorithms to determine where, when, and how ads should be delivered.

AI Bidirectional Advertising: This is a subset of programmatic purchasing, utilizing AI algorithms to automatically decide the bidding for each ad impression. These algorithms, based on extensive data such as user behavior, geographic location, and time, predict which ad displays are most likely to result in desired user actions, such as clicks or purchases.

Leveraging AI Technology to Optimize Ad Placement and Increase ROI

Target Audience Targeting: AI can analyze vast amounts of user data to identify specific user segments most likely to respond to ads. This allows advertisers to precisely target their intended audience, thereby enhancing ad effectiveness.

Real-time Optimization: AI algorithms can analyze ad performance metrics like click-through rates and conversion rates in real-time, automatically adjusting ad delivery strategies based on this data. This ensures ads are always placed in the optimal manner, thereby increasing ROI.

Budget Allocation: AI can predict which ad channels and strategies are most likely to yield optimal ad results and automatically allocate ad budgets, ensuring every dollar is spent in the most efficient manner.

Creative Optimization: AI can test various ad creatives, such as images, copy, and calls-to-action, and identify which creatives are most likely to engage users. This allows advertisers to ensure their ad content remains consistently appealing.

By constructing user profiles and employing AI technology for precise targeting, businesses can gain a deeper understanding of their users, enabling them to provide more personalized and tailored content and services. This not only enhances user satisfaction but also boosts conversion rates and increases sales revenue.

Application Cases

AI technology provides advertisers with powerful tools to enhance the precision and efficiency of ad placement. Through real-time analysis, automatic optimization, and precise targeting of the intended audience, advertisers can ensure that their ad placement strategies remain optimal, thereby boosting ad effectiveness and return on investment (ROI).

Here are some successful application cases demonstrating how prominent companies have leveraged AI technology to optimize bidirectional advertising and achieve significant results:

1. Coca-Cola:

Background: To enhance its ad effectiveness, Coca-Cola began using AI technology for ad placement.

Application: Coca-Cola employed AI to analyze the social media behaviors of its target audience, determining the best times and locations for ad placement.

Result: Through AI optimization, Coca-Cola witnessed an approximately 4x increase in ad click-through rates, significantly enhancing the efficiency of ad placement.

2. Booking.com:

Background: As a global leader in online travel and accommodation booking, Booking.com aimed to increase its ad conversion rates.

Application: Booking.com used AI technology to automatically tailor its ad creatives to match the preferences and behaviors of different users.

Result: Through AI-driven ad optimization, Booking.com achieved a roughly 15% increase in ad conversion rates.

3. Unilever:

Background: Unilever sought to improve the ad effectiveness of multiple brands and make more efficient use of its ad budget.

Application: Unilever employed AI technology for real-time ad effectiveness analysis and automatic adjustments to ad placement strategies.

Result: Through AI technology, Unilever successfully reduced its ad costs by around 30% while achieving significant improvements in ad effectiveness.

These cases showcase the immense potential of AI technology in the advertising field. Through precise targeting of the intended audience, real-time optimization, and automatic budget allocation, businesses can ensure their ad strategies are consistently optimal, thereby enhancing ad effectiveness and ROI.

AI Demand Forecasting and Inventory Management Optimization

As the complexity of global supply chains increases, demand forecasting and inventory management have become crucial factors for business success. AI technology offers innovative solutions to these challenges, aiding businesses in accurately predicting demand, optimizing inventory, and reducing costs.

Applications of AI in Sales Forecasting

Time Series Analysis: AI leverages historical sales data to identify sales trends and cyclic patterns, enabling predictions of future sales.

Deep Learning Models: By training neural network models, AI considers multiple factors such as seasonality, promotional activities, and market trends to enhance the accuracy of predictions.

Real-Time Data Analysis: AI performs real-time analysis of various data sources, such as social media trends, weather forecasts, and economic indicators, to adjust sales forecasts.

Combining AI Technology for Inventory Optimization and Cost Reduction

Dynamic Pricing: AI can automatically adjust prices based on demand forecasts, inventory levels, and other factors, thereby balancing demand and supply.

Intelligent Replenishment: AI algorithms can calculate optimal replenishment quantities and timings automatically, ensuring that inventory levels match forecasted demand while avoiding overstocking.

Inventory Classification: Utilizing AI technology, businesses can categorize inventory into different classes such as high-demand, low-demand, and seasonal products, enabling distinct inventory strategies for each category.

Reducing Inventory Costs: With more accurate demand forecasting and inventory optimization, companies can mitigate the risks of overstocking and stockouts, leading to reduced inventory costs and improved customer satisfaction.

AI technology provides powerful tools for demand forecasting and inventory management. Through enhanced accuracy in forecasting, dynamic pricing, and intelligent replenishment, businesses can ensure that their inventory strategies remain optimal, thereby boosting efficiency and lowering costs.

Application Case Studies

Amazon:

Background: As the world's largest e-commerce platform, Amazon processes millions of orders daily. To meet customer demands and maintain efficient operations, Amazon needs accurate demand forecasting and optimized inventory management.

Application: Amazon utilizes its own AI technology, such as Amazon Forecast, to predict product demand. Additionally, through its Kiva robot system, Amazon automates warehouse operations, enhancing inventory management efficiency.

Results: Through AI-driven demand forecasting and inventory optimization, Amazon successfully reduced the risks of overstocking and stockouts while increasing customer satisfaction and operational efficiency.

Walmart:

Background: As the largest global retailer, Walmart operates thousands of stores with extensive inventory. To boost sales and reduce costs, Walmart requires precise demand forecasting and inventory management.

Application: Walmart employs AI technology for real-time sales data analysis, automatically adjusting inventory strategies based on this data. Moreover, Walmart also utilizes AI technology for dynamic pricing, balancing demand and supply.

Results: Through AI technology, Walmart achieved increased sales, alongside reduced inventory costs and stockout risks.

3. Zara:

Background: As a fast-fashion brand, Zara needs to swiftly respond to market changes and adjust its product and inventory strategies in a timely manner.

Application: Zara employs AI technology to analyze social media and online search data, predicting fashion trends and product demand. Additionally, Zara also uses AI technology for inventory classification and intelligent replenishment, ensuring its inventory levels align with market demand.

Results: Through AI-driven demand forecasting and inventory optimization, Zara successfully mitigated the risks of overstocking, while increasing sales and customer satisfaction.

These case studies illustrate the immense potential of AI technology in inventory management. By means of more accurate demand forecasting, dynamic pricing, and intelligent replenishment, businesses can ensure their inventory strategies remain optimal, thereby enhancing efficiency and reducing costs.

AI-Driven Customer Service

With the advancement of technology, AI has become a pivotal tool in the realm of customer service. It not only enhances efficiency but also delivers more personalized services, thereby elevating customer satisfaction.

Application of AI Chatbots in Customer Support

Round-the-Clock Service: AI chatbots can provide service to customers around the clock without human intervention, catering to their needs anytime, anywhere.

Automated Issue Resolution: Chatbots swiftly identify customer issues and offer real-time solutions, thus increasing the efficiency of problem-solving.

Personalized Services: Based on customer historical data and behavior, AI chatbots can offer more personalized services and recommendations.

Multilingual Support: AI chatbots are capable of supporting multiple languages, extending their service to customers worldwide.

Enhancing Customer Satisfaction and Problem-Solving Efficiency with AI Technology

Sentiment Analysis: AI can analyze customers' language and behavior to identify their emotions and needs, thereby offering more suitable services.

Intelligent Routing: AI can automatically direct customer issues to the most appropriate customer service representative or department, thus improving the efficiency of problem resolution.

Automated Workflow: AI can automate customer service workflows such as order inquiries and refund processing, leading to increased efficiency and accuracy.

Continuous Learning: AI chatbots can continuously learn and improve, optimizing services based on customer feedback and behavior.

Successful Use Cases

Sephora: This beauty products retailer employs AI chatbots to offer customers product recommendations and makeup tutorials. Through AI technology, Sephora has effectively increased customer satisfaction and sales.

Bank of America: This bank utilizes its AI assistant, Erica, to provide customers with account inquiries, transactions, and other services. Erica not only enhances the efficiency of customer service but also saves the bank significant costs.

AI technology provides robust tools for customer service. With AI-driven chatbots and intelligent workflows, businesses can offer more efficient and personalized services, ultimately boosting customer satisfaction and loyalty.

Application of AI in E-commerce Data Analysis

The e-commerce industry has amassed a wealth of user data, including purchase history, browsing behavior, search records, and more. These data assets are valuable, but extracting meaningful insights from them is not straightforward. AI technology offers powerful tools for e-commerce data analysis, assisting businesses in gaining a better understanding of customers, optimizing operations, and boosting sales.

Utilizing AI Technology for E-commerce Data Mining and Analysis

User Behavior Analysis: AI can analyze users' browsing, search, and purchasing behaviors to identify their interests and needs, thereby providing more personalized services and recommendations.

Sales Forecasting: Based on historical data and market trends, AI can predict future sales and demand, aiding businesses in better inventory planning and promotional strategies.

Price Optimization: AI can analyze market and competitor data, automatically adjusting prices to enhance sales and profits.

Customer Segmentation: AI can automatically segment customers into different market segments, such as high-value customers, potential customers, etc., enabling tailored marketing strategies for each segment.

AI-Based E-commerce Data Visualization Tools and Techniques

Interactive Dashboards: AI-driven data visualization tools provide businesses with interactive dashboards that showcase key metrics such as sales, traffic, and conversion rates.

Data Exploration: With the aid of AI technology, companies can easily explore and analyze data, identifying potential opportunities and risks.

Intelligent Reports: AI can automatically generate reports, offering in-depth data analysis and recommendations to businesses.

Real-time Monitoring: AI-driven data visualization tools enable real-time monitoring of e-commerce platform operations, including traffic, sales, and inventory, helping companies rapidly respond to market changes.

Successful Application Cases

Alibaba: This globally leading e-commerce platform utilizes AI technology for data mining and analysis, aiding businesses in understanding customers, optimizing products, and boosting sales. Through AI-driven data visualization tools, Alibaba offers businesses profound market insights and recommendations.

Shopify: This e-commerce solutions provider employs AI technology to offer services such as sales forecasting, price optimization, and customer segmentation to businesses. Through AI-driven data analysis, Shopify assists businesses in enhancing sales and profits.

AI technology equips e-commerce data analysis with potent tools. With more accurate data mining and analysis, along with interactive data visualization, companies can better comprehend markets, optimize operations, and increase sales.

CHAPTER 3 AI EMPOWERS VIDEO ECONOMY

With the development of the internet, videos have become one of the most popular forms of content. From short video platforms to professional film and television production, video content is ubiquitous. AI technology has brought unprecedented opportunities and challenges to the video industry, playing a significant role in content creation, distribution, and promotion.

AI automatic editing technology and tutorial

What is AI Automatic Video Editing Technology?

AI automatic video editing technology utilizes machine learning and deep learning algorithms to automatically analyze, edit, and enhance video content. Compared to traditional manual editing, AI automatic video editing greatly improves efficiency, reduces costs, and provides more personalized content.

Key Features of AI Automatic Video Editing:

Intelligent Recognition: AI can automatically identify key frames, scenes, and objects within the video, enabling precise editing.

Content Enhancement: AI can optimize video content, pacing, and style based on user preferences and behavior.

Real-time Feedback: Users can preview AI-edited results in real time and make adjustments and refinements accordingly.

AI Automatic Video Editing Tutorial

Step 1: Choose a suitable AI automatic video editing tool or platform, such as Magisto, Adobe Sensei, and others.

Step 2: Import the original video files and set editing parameters, such as video length, style, and pacing.

Step 3: Activate the AI automatic video editing feature and wait for the AI to complete the analysis and editing process.

Step 4: Preview the editing results generated by AI and make minor adjustments and refinements as needed.

Step 5: Export the edited video files and share or publish them as desired.

Application Scenarios of AI Automatic Video Editing

Short Video Production: Utilizing AI automatic video editing, users can quickly create engaging short video content for popular platforms like TikTok, Kuaishou, and others.

Film and Television Post-Production: For professional filmmakers and producers, AI automatic video editing can offer more efficient and precise editing solutions, enhancing the quality and efficiency of production.

Corporate Promotional Videos: Enterprises can leverage AI automatic video editing to create high-quality promotional videos, elevating brand awareness and influence.

AI technology has brought significant opportunities and challenges to the video economy. From content creation to distribution and promotion, AI plays a crucial role. For video creators and businesses alike, mastering and applying AI technology has become a key factor in enhancing competitiveness.

Working Principles of Modern AI Video Editing Tools

Modern AI video editing tools combine technologies such as deep learning, computer vision, and natural language processing to provide intelligent solutions for video editing. The following outlines the basic working principles of these tools:

Data Training

Training Dataset: AI video editing tools initially require a large dataset of videos for training. These datasets encompass various types of video content, including movies, advertisements, news reports, and more.

Feature Extraction: AI algorithms extract key features from these videos, such as scene transitions, object movements, facial expressions, audio rhythms, and more.

Model Training: Utilizing these features, AI algorithms train a model capable of automatically recognizing key frames, scenes, and events within the videos.

Video Analysis

Scene Recognition: AI tools automatically identify different scenes within videos, such as indoor, outdoor, day, night, and so on.

Object and Person Recognition: Through computer vision techniques, AI can recognize objects and individuals within the video, such as vehicles, buildings, animals, and faces.

Audio Analysis: AI tools also analyze the audio content of the video, including dialogue, background music, sound effects, etc., to determine the video's rhythm and emotional tone.

Automatic Video Editing

Content Selection: Based on the results of video analysis, AI tools automatically select key content and scenes for editing.

Editing Strategy: Users can set editing parameters such as video length, style, and rhythm. AI will then perform editing according to these parameters.

Real-time Preview: During the editing process, users can preview AI's editing results in real-time and make adjustments and optimizations.

Output and Sharing

Format Conversion: AI tools can automatically convert video formats such as MP4, AVI, MOV, etc., to meet different playback and sharing needs.

Intelligent Compression: To improve video transmission speed and playback quality, AI tools can perform intelligent compression to reduce the video file size.

Sharing and Publishing: Users can directly share and publish videos from AI tools, such as uploading to platforms like YouTube, Vimeo, or sharing on social media.

Successful Case Studies

BBC's Experiment: BBC conducted an experimental project using AI technology to automatically edit a documentary. By analyzing the audio, visual, and metadata content from the original footage, AI successfully edited several hours of material into a coherent 15-minute short film.

TikTok's Intelligent Editing: TikTok, the short video platform, employs AI technology to assist users in automatically editing and enhancing video content, enabling the rapid creation of engaging short videos.

Introduction to Typical Tools

Magisto:

Overview: Magisto is an online video editing tool that utilizes AI technology to assist users in automatically cutting, editing, and enhancing video content.

Features: Users simply need to upload their original video and audio files, choose an editing style, and Magisto will automatically create a professionally quality video for them.

Use Cases: Suitable for both personal and business users, especially those without prior video editing experience.

Adobe Sensei:

Overview: Adobe Sensei is Adobe's AI and machine learning platform integrated into multiple Adobe products, including Premiere Pro.

Features: Sensei can automatically identify and tag key frames, scenes, and objects in videos, helping users quickly locate and edit the desired content.

Use Cases: Suitable for professional video editors and designers who require integration with other Adobe products.

Clipchamp:

Overview: Clipchamp is an online video editing and compression tool that offers various AI-powered features, such as smart editing, background removal, and video enhancement.

Features: Users can directly use Clipchamp in their web browsers without the need to download or install any software.

How to Efficiently Perform Video Editing Using AI

Utilizing AI for efficient video editing not only saves a significant amount of time and effort but also enhances the quality of videos and audience engagement. Here are the steps and suggestions on how to efficiently perform video editing using AI:

Choose an Appropriate AI Video Editing Tool

Based on your needs and budget, select a suitable AI video editing tool or platform, such as Magisto, Clipchamp, or Adobe Sensei.

Import Original Video Footage

Import your original video files into the AI video editing tool.

Advanced tools allow you to import videos from various sources, such as cameras, smartphones, or cloud storage.

Set Editing Parameters

Set editing parameters based on your goals and audience, such as video length, style, pacing, and music.

Some tools provide preset editing templates to help you get started quickly.

Activate AI Auto Editing

Once you've set all the parameters, you can activate the AI auto editing feature.

AI algorithms will analyze your video content, identify key frames, scenes, and events, and perform editing according to your settings.

Preview and Fine-Tune

After AI completes the editing, you can preview the edited result.

If necessary, you can fine-tune and optimize, such as adjusting the order of clips, adding transition effects, or including text titles.

Export and Sharing

Once you are satisfied with the edited result, you can export the video file.

You can choose different formats and resolutions to meet various playback and sharing needs.

Some tools also offer direct sharing to social media or video platforms such as YouTube, Vimeo, or TikTok.

Utilizing AI for Analysis and Optimization

In addition to auto editing, some advanced AI video tools also provide video analysis and optimization features.

For instance, they can automatically identify problematic areas in the video, such as blurriness, shaky footage, or overexposure, and perform automatic fixes.

Some tools also offer audience engagement analysis, helping you understand which parts of the video are most popular and which areas need improvement.

Conclusion

Using AI for video editing not only enhances efficiency but also improves the quality of videos and audience engagement. Whether you're an individual creator or a professional video production team, you can benefit from AI video editing tools.

AI-Enhanced Filters, Effects, and Post-Processing

The application of AI technology in video post-processing has become increasingly popular, especially in the realms of filters, effects, and video enhancement. Here are the applications and techniques of AI in these areas:

AI Filters

Automatic Color Correction: AI can analyze a video's color balance and exposure automatically, then perform adjustments to make the video look more natural and professional.

Style Transfer: Utilizing deep learning techniques, AI can transfer a certain style (such as that of famous paintings or specific photography styles) onto a video, creating unique visual effects.

AI Effects

Intelligent Background Replacement: Through computer vision technology, AI can recognize foreground and background elements in a video and replace the background with other scenes or images, without the need for a green screen.

Automatic Object Tracking: AI can automatically track objects or individuals in a video and add various effects such as dynamic blurring, halos, or animated labels.

Video Beautification and Enhancement

Super-Resolution: AI can upscale low-resolution videos to higher resolutions while preserving clarity and details.

Video Denoising: AI can identify and remove noise and interference from videos automatically, resulting in clearer video quality.

Video Stabilization: Utilizing AI technology, shaky videos can be automatically stabilized, giving them a smoother and more professional appearance.

AI Applications in Video Post-Processing: Case Studies

NVIDIA's AI Video Enhancement: NVIDIA has developed AI technology that automatically enhances video resolution, removes noise, and stabilizes videos. This technology has been integrated into

NVIDIA's graphics cards and software, providing powerful post-processing tools for professional video producers.

AI Effects on TikTok: The short-video platform TikTok offers a variety of AI-driven effects and filters, including style transfer, background replacement, and object tracking. These effects assist users in quickly creating captivating short videos.

Technologies for Video Beautification and Enhancement Using AI

Deep Learning: Deep learning is the fundamental technology behind AI video post-processing. It can automatically learn and extract features from videos, enabling various processing and optimizations.

Computer Vision: Computer vision technology assists AI in automatically identifying and tracking objects, people, and scenes within videos, allowing for the implementation of various effects and filters.

Natural Language Processing: Some advanced AI video tools also offer features such as voice recognition and automatic subtitle generation, facilitating the rapid creation of multilingual videos.

AI-Generated Virtual Character Videos

With the advancement of technology, AI can now generate not only static images and audio but also complete virtual character videos. This technology offers boundless possibilities for content creators, advertisers, game developers, and more.

Development and Application of Virtual Character Generation Technology

Early Techniques: In the early stages of AI-generated virtual characters, traditional 3D modeling and animation techniques were primarily relied upon. These methods required a significant amount of manual work and artistic creativity.

Advances in Deep Learning: As deep learning and neural networks advanced, researchers began using these technologies to generate virtual characters. For instance, Generative Adversarial Networks (GANs) can produce highly realistic facial images.

Complete Virtual Character Videos: Nowadays, by combining deep learning with traditional 3D techniques, AI can generate full virtual character videos, encompassing facial expressions, body movements, and even voice.

Application Areas: Virtual character videos have found widespread application in fields such as film, advertising, gaming, and virtual reality. For instance, filmmakers can employ AI-generated virtual actors, while advertisers can create customized virtual spokespersons.

How AI Ensures Realism and Naturalness of Virtual Characters

High-Resolution Generation: Through the utilization of large neural networks and extensive training data, AI can generate high-resolution and high-quality virtual character images.

Detail Capture: AI can capture and simulate minute details of characters, such as skin texture, hair, and reflections in the eyes.

Motion and Expression Simulation: By combining deep learning with traditional animation techniques, AI can simulate natural movements and expressions of characters. For example, AI can analyze real human facial expressions and transfer them onto virtual characters.

Voice Synchronization: Some advanced AI tools offer voice synchronization capabilities to ensure the perfect alignment of a virtual character's lip movements with their speech.

Realism Testing: After generating virtual character videos, realism testing can be conducted to assess their quality. This evaluation typically involves real human participants who assess the realism and naturalness of the virtual characters.

In Conclusion: AI-generated virtual character videos offer limitless possibilities for content creators, but they also raise ethical and societal concerns such as deep fakes and the spread of misinformation. Therefore, caution is necessary when using this technology, ensuring its application for legitimate and beneficial purposes.

76

How to Create High-Converting AI Video Tutorials

In the realm of digital marketing, videos have emerged as an incredibly effective form of content. By harnessing AI technology, we can craft videos that are more engaging and targeted, ultimately boosting both viewer retention and conversion rates. The following are recommendations and steps on how to create high-converting AI video tutorials, aligned with North American practices, while retaining the original meaning and format:

Define Objectives and Audience

Before diving into the creative process, it's crucial to clearly establish the objectives of your video. Is it intended to enhance brand awareness, promote a product/service, or provide educational content to the audience?

Gain an understanding of your target audience. Utilize AI tools to analyze audience interests, behaviors, and preferences. This analysis will help you generate content that is tailored to their specific needs.

Craft Targeted Content

Leverage AI technology to analyze extensive datasets, including search queries, social media interactions, and website browsing behaviors. This analysis enables you to identify the most intriguing topics and content for your audience.

Based on these insights, create content that is specific, relevant, and resonates with your audience.

Optimizing Video Quality and Format

Utilize AI tools to automatically adjust video color, brightness, and contrast, enhancing its professional appearance.

Based on the audience's devices and network conditions, automatically adapt the video's resolution and encoding format to ensure a seamless playback experience.

Craft Compelling Titles and Descriptions

Utilize AI technology to analyze audience search queries and interactions, automatically generating captivating titles and descriptions, thus increasing video click-through rates.

Conduct A/B Testing with AI

Generate multiple versions of the video, featuring different titles, descriptions, or cover images.

Utilize AI tools to conduct A/B testing, determining which version of the video garners higher view rates and conversion rates.

Facilitate Video Distribution and Sharing

Utilize AI technology to analyze audience social media interactions, identifying optimal posting times and platforms.

Automatically push videos to the audience's most active social media platforms, such as Facebook, YouTube, or TikTok.

Analysis and Optimization

Employ AI tools to automatically analyze video view data, including watch duration, bounce rates, and conversion rates.

Based on this data, continually optimize video content, format, and promotional strategies to enhance effectiveness.

Successful Application Cases

Personalized Recommendations by Netflix

Netflix employs sophisticated AI algorithms to analyze users' viewing habits and provide personalized movie and TV show recommendations. However, that's not all. Netflix also employs AI technology to automatically generate cover images for video previews. These images are tailored to each user's viewing history and preferences, enhancing click-through rates and watch time.

AI-Driven Advertising by Coca-Cola

During the 2017 Grammy Awards, Coca-Cola launched a series of AI-generated ads. These ads utilized natural language processing technology to analyze real-time conversations on social media and dynamically generate ad content relevant to these discussions. This approach ensured the relevance and timeliness of the ads, thereby increasing audience engagement.

L'Oréal's AI Beauty Assistant

Cosmetics giant L'Oréal introduced an AI video assistant named "Beauty For All." This assistant analyzes users' uploaded selfies and recommends the most suitable makeup and skincare products for them. Additionally, the assistant offers video tutorials on how to use these products. This personalized video content significantly boosts user purchase conversion rates.

AI Video Editing by the NBA

NBA employs AI technology to automatically edit highlights from games and publish these videos on social media and their official website. This approach not only enhances the efficiency of video production but also ensures the timeliness and relevance of the content.

AR Video Application by IKEA

Home furnishing leader IKEA launched an augmented reality video application that allows users to virtually place furniture in their homes. This application uses AI technology to analyze users' home environments and recommend the most suitable furniture styles and layouts. This interactive video experience greatly increases user purchase intent.

These successful application cases demonstrate that both large corporations and small startups can leverage AI technology to create and promote video content, ultimately boosting view rates and conversion rates. These cases also offer valuable insights and inspiration for other industries and fields.

CHAPTER 4: AI EMPOWERING SOCIAL MARKETING

With the widespread use of social media, brands and businesses are increasingly relying on these platforms for marketing and engaging with customers. AI technology provides powerful tools for social media marketing, helping companies interact more effectively with their audiences, increase brand awareness, and boost sales conversion rates.

Sharing of AI social media operation skills

Content Optimization: AI can analyze audience engagement data and automatically recommend the most popular content formats and topics, helping operators create more appealing content.

Smart Scheduling: By analyzing the audience's online activity times, AI can automatically determine the optimal posting times, increasing the exposure of content.

Automatic Responses: Utilizing AI chatbots to automatically respond to user comments and private messages, enhancing user satisfaction while saving on customer service costs.

How AI helps social media operators improve efficiency

Automated Tasks: AI tools can automatically complete repetitive tasks such as content distribution, comment responses, and data analysis, allowing operators to have more time to focus on strategic and creative work.

Predictive Analytics: AI can predict which content or activities are most likely to succeed, assisting operators in planning and promoting content more effectively.

Leveraging AI for social media content planning and publishing

Content Generation: AI tools, such as GPT-3, can automatically generate high-quality textual content, providing a continuous supply of content for social media.

Image and Video Optimization: AI can automatically adjust the size and format of images and videos, ensuring smooth playback on various devices and network environments.

Applications of AI in Hotspot Monitoring and Keyword Extraction

Hotspot Monitoring: AI tools can monitor popular topics and trends on social media in real-time, helping businesses adjust their strategies promptly to seize marketing opportunities.

Keyword Extraction: By analyzing user comments and feedback on social media, AI can automatically extract keywords and phrases, assisting businesses in understanding audience needs and concerns.

AI technology has brought revolutionary changes to social media marketing. From content planning to user engagement, AI is helping businesses market more efficiently and precisely. With further advancements in AI technology, we can expect social media marketing to become even smarter and more personalized.

AI Community Customer Management User Guide

With the rise of community marketing, community customer management has become a key factor in the success of brands and businesses. AI technology has brought unprecedented opportunities to community management, assisting businesses in interacting more effectively with community members, thereby enhancing customer satisfaction and loyalty.

Application and advantages of AI in community management

Automatic Responses: AI chatbots can provide instant responses and support to community members 24/7, enhancing user satisfaction while also saving on the cost of human customer service.

Emotion Analysis: AI tools can automatically analyze user comments and feedback within the community, helping businesses understand and respond to the emotions and needs of community members in a timely manner.

Predictive Analytics: AI can predict which content or activities are most likely to be welcomed by community members, assisting businesses in planning and promoting content more effectively.

Personalized Recommendations: Based on the behavior and preferences of community members, AI can automatically recommend relevant content and activities, increasing user engagement and activity.

How to use AI for accurate community customer management

Building User Profiles: Utilizing AI tools to collect and analyze behavioral data of community members, constructing detailed user profiles to help businesses gain a deeper understanding of the needs and preferences of community members.

Intelligent Segmentation: AI can automatically categorize community members into different groups, such as new users, active users, and inactive users, assisting businesses in devising distinct marketing strategies for different segments.

Automated Marketing: Leveraging AI tools like Mailchimp or HubSpot to automatically send personalized emails and messages, enhancing the conversion rates of marketing campaigns.

Smart Monitoring: AI tools can monitor user behavior and interactions within the community in real-time, helping businesses promptly identify and address potential issues and risks.

AI technology has brought revolutionary changes to community customer management. From building user profiles to personalized recommendations, AI is aiding businesses in managing communities more efficiently and with greater precision. With further advancements in AI technology, we can expect community customer management to become even more intelligent and personalized.

AI community customer management application cases

Case 1: Intelligent Community Q&A Chatbot

Background: A large tech community with millions of registered users faces a constant influx of technical questions and discussions every day.

Solution: The community introduced an AI-based chatbot dedicated to answering common user questions. The bot automatically provides users with the most relevant answers by analyzing historical Q&A data.

Results: The chatbot successfully resolved 80% of common questions, significantly reducing the workload of community administrators while enhancing user satisfaction.

Case 2: AI Sentiment Analysis Tool

Background: A health and fitness community where users frequently share their fitness experiences and insights.

Solution: The community utilizes an AI sentiment analysis tool to automatically analyze user comments and feedback, gaining real-time insights into user emotional fluctuations.

Results: Community administrators can promptly identify and address negative emotions, mitigating potential risks and crises. Additionally, based on users' positive emotions, they can recommend relevant fitness courses and products.

Case 3: AI Personalized Recommendation System

Background: A literary community with a vast collection of novels and stories.

90

Solution: The community introduced an AI personalized recommendation system that automatically suggests the most relevant novels and stories based on users' reading history and preferences.

Results: Users' reading time and activity significantly increased, leading to a marked improvement in user engagement and retention within the community.

Case 4: AI Intelligent Segmentation Tool

Background: A photography community with users from different countries and regions, having varying levels of photography skills and experience.

Solution: The community employs an AI intelligent segmentation tool to automatically categorize users into three groups: beginners, intermediate, and advanced. Customized content and activities are provided for each group.

Results: Users feel that the community is more caring and understanding of their needs, leading to increased user engagement and satisfaction within the community.

These cases demonstrate the applications and value of AI technology in community customer management. By harnessing AI technology effectively, communities can interact with users more efficiently, enhancing user satisfaction and loyalty.

AI user interaction and consultation automation applications

In today's digital era, users expect real-time and seamless interactions with businesses. To meet this demand, many companies have already begun adopting AI technologies, especially AI chatbots and automated response systems, to enhance the efficiency of user interactions and inquiries.

Application of AI chatbot and automatic reply system

Instant Responses: Whether it's day or night, AI chatbots can provide 24/7 online support to users, ensuring that user questions and concerns are addressed promptly.

Intelligent Recognition: Through natural language processing technology, AI chatbots can accurately identify user queries and provide relevant answers or solutions.

Multi-Tasking: Unlike traditional customer service, AI chatbots can handle inquiries from multiple users simultaneously, significantly enhancing response speed and efficiency.

Leveraging AI to improve the efficiency of user interactions and consultations

Personalized Experience: Based on user's historical data and behavior, AI systems can provide each user with a personalized interactive experience, such as recommending relevant products or services.

Automated Processes: For common issues or requests, AI systems can automatically handle processing, such as order inquiries, refund requests, etc., without the need for human intervention.

Continuous Learning: AI chatbots have the ability to self-learn, continuously optimizing their responses and strategies based on user feedback and interaction history.

Applications

Case 1: AI Customer Service Assistant for an E-commerce Website

Background: A large e-commerce website faces a high volume of user inquiries and issues every day.

Solution: The website introduced an AI chatbot dedicated to answering common user questions, such as order status and return policies.

Results: The chatbot successfully resolved 90% of common questions, significantly reducing the workload of customer service agents while enhancing user satisfaction.

Case 2: AI Advisory Assistant for a Bank

Background: A large bank receives a high volume of customer inquiries and issues every day.

Solution: The bank developed an AI advisory assistant that can provide customers with instant loan advice, exchange rate inquiries, and other services.

Results: Customer inquiry efficiency significantly improved, and the bank also saved a substantial amount of manpower costs.。

These cases demonstrate the applications and value of AI technology in user interaction and inquiry automation. By utilizing AI technology effectively, businesses can interact with users more efficiently, delivering better service and support.

Social e-commerce uses AI technology to increase sales

Social commerce combines the interactivity of social media with the shopping functionality of e-commerce, offering users a brand-new shopping experience. With the advancement of AI technology, an increasing number of social commerce platforms are starting to adopt AI to enhance sales and user satisfaction.

Application cases of AI in social e-commerce

Personalized Recommendations: Based on users' shopping history, browsing behavior, and social interactions, AI systems can offer users personalized product recommendations, boosting conversion rates.

Case: A certain social commerce platform introduced an AI recommendation algorithm that analyzes users' likes, comments, and sharing behavior to recommend the most relevant products to users. As a result, the platform's conversion rate increased by 30%.

Intelligent Customer Support: AI chatbots can provide users with 24/7 online support, answering their questions and offering shopping advice.

Case: A certain social commerce platform utilizes AI chatbots to provide users with real-time shopping consultations and after-sales support. User satisfaction has significantly increased, and return rates have decreased.

Intelligent Advertising Placement: Through AI technology, social commerce platforms can target advertising more precisely, ensuring that ad content aligns with users' interests and needs.

Case: A certain social commerce platform uses AI technology to automatically analyze users' social interactions and shopping behavior, delivering the most relevant ads to each user. Click-through rates and conversion rates have both seen significant improvements.

How to use AI technology to increase sales in social e-commerce

Data Analysis: Through AI technology, social commerce platforms can delve into user data to understand shopping habits, interests, and needs, thereby offering more precise products and services.

Automated Marketing: AI technology can assist social commerce platforms in automating marketing activities, such as sending personalized promotional messages and reminding users about items in their shopping carts.

Enhanced User Experience: AI technology can help social commerce platforms provide a smoother and more personalized shopping experience, including intelligent search and virtual try-ons.

Applications

Personalized Recommendation System of Xiaohongshu

Xiaohongshu is a well-known social commerce platform that utilizes AI technology to provide personalized content recommendations for users. By analyzing users' browsing history, likes, and comments, the AI system can recommend the most relevant content and products to each user. This not only increases user engagement but also significantly boosts conversion rates and sales revenue.

Pinduoduo's Intelligent Advertising Placement

Pinduoduo is a large Chinese social commerce platform that employs AI technology for intelligent advertising placement. By analyzing users' shopping behavior and social interactions, the AI system can deliver the most relevant ads to each user. This not only increases ad click-through rates but also significantly improves conversion rates and ROI.

98

Zhuanzhuan's intelligent customer service system

Zhuanzhuan is a second-hand goods trading platform that utilizes AI chatbots to provide users with 24/7 online support. Whether it's product inquiries, transaction processes, or post-sale issues, the AI chatbot can offer users timely and accurate answers, significantly enhancing user satisfaction.

Vipshop's AI Data Analysis

Vipshop is a flash sale e-commerce platform that utilizes AI technology for in-depth data analysis. By analyzing users' shopping habits, search keywords, and click behavior, the AI system can provide each user with the most relevant product recommendations. This not only enhances the user's shopping experience but also significantly increases sales revenue.

Summary

These application examples showcase the tremendous potential of AI technology in social e-commerce. Whether it's content recommendations, advertising, customer support, or data analysis, AI technology can provide robust support to social e-commerce platforms, helping them improve efficiency, enhance user experiences, and increase sales revenue.

AI technology opens up new possibilities for social e-commerce. By harnessing AI technology correctly, social e-commerce platforms can not only offer more personalized and satisfying shopping experiences but also significantly boost sales and profits. With the further development of AI technology, we can expect the future of social e-commerce to become even more intelligent and efficient.

CHAPTER 5 AI COMMERCIALIZATION PATH

Commercial Analysis of the AI Knowledge Subscription Model

Current State and Trends in the AI Knowledge Subscription Market

Market Background: In the digital age, there has been a growing demand for knowledge, giving rise to the knowledge subscription market. With technological advancements, AI has begun to make inroads into this field, bringing revolutionary changes to knowledge subscription.

User Profiles: Modern users prioritize time efficiency, seeking quick and accurate access to the knowledge they need. Furthermore, they value personalized learning experiences and are no longer satisfied with one-size-fits-all content.

Role of AI: AI technology can deeply analyze user behavior and preferences, providing them with more precise content recommendations. Additionally, AI can assist knowledge creators in producing content more efficiently to meet users' personalized demands.

Example: Coursera, an online education platform, has already started using AI technology to offer personalized course recommendations to users. Based on users' learning history, browsing behavior, and feedback, AI algorithms predict courses that might interest users and recommend them accordingly.

Enhancing the Value of Knowledge Subscription Products with AI

AI Empowers Content Creation: AI can assist knowledge creators in automatically generating articles, videos, and other content, significantly improving production efficiency. For instance, OpenAI's CHATGPT can help authors auto-generate articles or tutorials. Grammarly, an AI-based writing assistant, offers real-time grammar and style suggestions to users, enhancing the quality of their writing.

Personalized Recommendations: Based on user behavior and preferences, AI systems can provide personalized knowledge content recommendations for each user. For example, a knowledge subscription platform utilizes AI technology to recommend a series of courses highly tailored to users' interests and needs, greatly boosting user conversion rates. Udemy, an online course marketplace, has already started using AI technology to offer personalized course recommendations. AI algorithms recommend the most relevant courses for users based on their learning history and search behavior.

Intelligent Interaction and Q&A: AI chatbots can provide real-time Q&A support to users, helping them resolve learning-related queries. For instance, an online education platform introduced an AI teaching assistant feature, offering users 24/7 online Q&A services, significantly enhancing user satisfaction. Example: Duolingo, a language learning app, uses AI technology to provide personalized learning paths and real-time Q&A support to users.

Knowledge Graphs and Path Planning: AI technology can assist users in constructing personalized learning paths, ensuring they can systematically and efficiently acquire knowledge. For example, a knowledge subscription platform employs AI technology to generate a personalized knowledge graph for each user, aiding them in purposeful learning. Example: Khan Academy, a platform offering free online courses, has begun using AI technology to provide users with

104

personalized learning paths. Based on users' learning progress and test scores, AI algorithms recommend the next steps in their learning journey.

AI technology brings significant opportunities to the knowledge subscription market. By deeply analyzing user needs and behavior, AI can provide knowledge subscription platforms with more precise and efficient services, meeting the high standards of modern users. With the further development of AI technology, we have reason to believe that the knowledge subscription market will have a more brilliant future.

Discussion on providing AI generation services

Market Demand and Applications of AI Generation Services

Market Background: With the increasing maturity of AI technology, more and more businesses and individuals are seeking AI generation services to improve work efficiency, reduce costs, or create new value.

Applications

Content Creation: Such as AI writing, image generation, music composition, etc.

Data Analysis: AI can automatically generate reports, providing businesses with in-depth insights.

Design and Art: Such as AI assisting designers in generating design sketches or providing creative inspiration for artists.

Gaming and Entertainment: AI-generated characters, scenes, or storylines.

Example: DeepArt.io, which is an AI-based art creation platform, allows users to upload images, and AI automatically generates images in various artistic styles.

How to Provide High-Quality AI Generation Services to Customers

Understanding Customer Needs: Engage in deep communication with customers to understand their specific requirements, expected outcomes, and application scenarios.

Selecting the Right AI Model: Based on the customer's needs, choose the most suitable AI model. For example, for text generation, options like GPT-3 or BERT can be considered; for image generation, options like DALL-E or GAN may be appropriate.

Data Preparation: Provide high-quality training data to AI models to ensure accurate and engaging content generation.

Continuous Optimization: Collect customer feedback and continuously refine AI models to improve the quality of generated content.

Offering Personalized Services: Provide personalized AI generation solutions for different customers to meet their unique needs.

Example: Jasper Studios, a company that offers AI music composition services, engages in in-depth communication with customers to understand their musical tastes and requirements. They then use AI technology to create unique music compositions for their customers.

AI generation services provide significant value to businesses and individuals. They not only enhance work efficiency and reduce costs but also create entirely new experiences for users. To ensure the delivery of high-quality services, service providers need to deeply understand customer needs, choose appropriate AI models, and continually optimize service quality.

Recommendations for AI Technology Capabilities Export

Opportunities and Challenges of AI Technology Outsourcing and Collaboration

Opportunities::

- arket Demand Growth: With the proliferation of AI technology, more and more businesses and organizations are seeking external collaborations to quickly acquire AI capabilities.
- Technology Sharing: Through external collaborations, companies can gain access to the latest AI technologies and knowledge.

- Cost Efficiency: Outsourcing or collaborating can help companies reduce research and development costs and achieve rapid technology implementation.

Challenges:

- Technology Confidentiality: Ensuring that technology is not leaked or misused.
- Collaboration Standards: Establishing responsibilities and rights for both parties to ensure smooth collaboration.
- Quality Control: Ensuring the quality and effectiveness of external collaborations or outsourcing.

How to Ensure the Quality and Effectiveness of AI Technology Outputs

Define Clear Collaboration Objectives: Clearly define the goals and expected outcomes of the technical outputs with your collaborators.

Choose the Right Partners: Select experienced and capable partners to ensure the quality of the technology outputs.

Establish Evaluation Mechanisms: Regularly assess the effectiveness of the technology outputs and make adjustments based on feedback.

Provide Technical Support: Offer technical training and support to your partners to ensure the correct application of the technology.

Protect Technology Intellectual Property: Sign confidentiality agreements with partners to safeguard against technology leaks or misuse.

Example: IBM Watson collaborates with various enterprises, applying Watson technology in various domains such as healthcare and finance. IBM not only provides the technology but also offers training and support to partners, ensuring the quality and effectiveness of the technology outputs.

AI technology outputs present new business opportunities for companies but also come with challenges. Companies need to define clear objectives, select suitable partners, establish evaluation mechanisms, provide technical support, and protect intellectual property to ensure the quality and effectiveness of technology outputs.

Designing AI-Based Information Service Products

Design Principles for AI Information Service Products

User-Centric Approach: Always start with user needs to ensure that AI technology truly delivers value to users.

Data-Driven: Make full use of data to train and optimize AI models, ensuring the accuracy and real-time capabilities of information services.

Privacy Protection: Prioritize user privacy when collecting and processing user data, ensuring data security.

Continuous Iteration: Continuously improve and update the product as technology advances and user needs change.

Providing More Personalized and Precise Information Services Using AI

Personalized Recommendations: Analyzing user behavior and preferences to offer personalized information recommendations.

Smart Search: Leveraging AI technology to provide more accurate and faster search results.

Automatic Content Generation: Using AI technology to automatically generate news, reports, and other content, delivering real-time information updates to users.

AI Startup Business Model Case Study

Case: DeepL

Background: DeepL is an AI-based translation service startup.

Business Model: Offering free online translation services and providing paid API access services to enterprise clients.

AI Application: Utilizing deep learning technology to deliver more precise translation results compared to traditional translation tools.

Success Factors: High-quality translation results, a user-friendly interface, and robust technical support.

Designing AI-based information service products requires adhering to certain principles to ensure that the products genuinely meet user needs. By harnessing AI technology, more personalized and precise information services can be provided to users. Additionally, analyzing successful AI startup company cases can offer valuable references and insights for businesses.

CHAPTER 6 PRACTICAL CASES

AI Empowering Individual Users to Quickly Generate Income

AI-Powered Writing

Case: Personal Blog Writing

a. Choose a Topic and Direction:

For beginners, start by defining the theme of your blog. This can be your interests, expertise, or current trending topics. For example, AI, healthy eating, travel experiences, etc.

b. Initial Brainstorming:

List down the main points or structure you want to write about on paper or your computer.

c. Use AI Tools to Generate an Initial Draft:

Open ChatGPT, input your topic and initial thoughts.

ChatGPT will generate an initial draft for you, which can serve as the framework for your article.

d. Revise and Polish:

Read the initial draft generated by ChatGPT and supplement it with your knowledge and research. Use Grammarly for grammar and style corrections. Grammarly automatically detects grammar errors and provides editing suggestions in your article.

e. Publish and Promote:

Choose a blogging platform like WordPress, Blogger, or Medium for publishing.

Share the link to your article on social media to attract more readers.

f. Earn Income:

Place advertisements on your blog, such as Google AdSense, and earn income whenever someone clicks on the ads.

Offer paid subscriptions where readers pay a fee to access your exclusive content or in-depth analysis.

Consider offering your own courses or columns on knowledge payment platforms like Ximalaya and Dedao to share your knowledge and expertise.

AI Empowering Image Creation

Case: Individual Illustrator

a. Determine Your Creative Direction:

For beginners, start by defining your illustration style and theme. This can be pop culture, natural landscapes, abstract art, or any other theme that interests you.

b. Initial Concept and Sketch:

Draw your initial concept or sketch on paper or using digital drawing tools. This will serve as a reference for DALL-E.

c. Use AI Tools to Generate Illustrations:

Open DALL-E and upload your sketch or describe your concept. DALL-E will generate a series of illustrations related to your concept. Choose your favorites from the generated options.

d. Add Artistic Styles:

Use DeepArt to upload your selected illustrations and choose an artistic style, such as Van Gogh, Picasso, or the style of any other famous artist.

DeepArt will automatically apply the chosen artistic style to your illustrations, giving them an artistic flair.

e. Optimize and Refine:

As needed, you can use other image editing tools to further optimize and refine the generated illustrations, such as adjusting colors, adding details, etc.

f. Publish and Sell:

You can upload your works to stock image websites like Shutterstock, Getty Images, etc. You'll earn income whenever someone purchases your illustrations.

Additionally, you can sell your illustrations as red envelope covers, T-shirt designs, phone wallpapers, and more, or showcase them on social media to attract fans and orders.

By combining your own ideas with the capabilities of AI tools, you can rapidly create unique illustrations and generate income through various channels.

AI Enhancing Video Production

Case: Individual Vlogger

a. Video Content Planning:

For beginners, start by defining the theme of your Vlog. This can be daily life, travel, food, skill sharing, and more.

List the main content and structure you want to showcase or talk about in your Vlog.

b. Shoot Raw Footage:

Use a camera or smartphone for shooting. Ensure the content you capture is rich enough for later editing.

c. Video Editing Using AI Tools:

Import your raw footage into Magisto.

Choose a template or style that suits your Vlog theme; Magisto will automatically edit your video, adding background music, transitions, and other effects.

d. Add Effects or Replace Characters:

If you want to add fun effects or replace characters in your video, you can use Deepfake tools.

For example, you can replace your face with that of a celebrity or add some animated effects.

e. Optimize and Enhance:

As needed, you can use other video editing tools to further optimize and enhance the generated video, such as adjusting the volume, adding subtitles, and more.

f. Publish and Promote:

Select a video platform like YouTube, Bilibili, etc., for publishing.

Share your video links on social media to attract more viewers.

Set appropriate titles, descriptions, and tags for your video to make it easier for search engines and viewers to find.

g. Generate Revenue:

Enable the advertising revenue feature on your video platform.

You'll earn ad revenue every time someone watches your videos.

You can also consider offering paid content like tutorials, exclusive behind-the-scenes footage, etc., for viewers to pay a fee to access.

AI Assisting Individual Translators

Case: Individual Translator

a. Receiving Translation Tasks:

You can accept translation orders on various translation platforms or receive translation requests from clients through your own social media, website, and other channels.

b. Text Preparation:

Organize the text that needs translation, remove unnecessary formatting, and ensure the text is clear.

c. Initial Translation Using AI Tools:

Input the organized text into DeepL for translation. DeepL provides more accurate and natural translation results, especially for European languages.

Save the translation results from DeepL.

d. Proofreading Using Google Translate:

Input the translation results from DeepL into Google Translate for comparison. Google Translate has extensive language support and a vast corpus, which can help you identify and correct errors or inaccuracies in the translation.

e. Manual Verification and Optimization:

Carefully read through the translated text to ensure it fits the context and flows naturally.

For content involving professional terminology or cultural context, make appropriate adjustments and optimizations.

f. Submitting the Translation:

Submit the completed translation to the client and charge the corresponding fee.

Offer some post-translation services, such as revising the translation content or addressing the client's questions.

g. Earning Revenue:

You can set your own pricing standards on major translation platforms or offer paid translation services on your website.

In addition to direct translation fees, you can provide value-added services like specialized domain translation or rush services to increase your earnings.

AI Empowering Social Media Marketing

Case: Personal Brand Promotion

a. Define Brand Positioning and Target Audience:

Before starting your social media marketing efforts, it's essential to clarify what your brand represents and the type of audience you aim to attract.

b. Create and Curate Content:

Create relevant content such as articles, images, videos, etc., based on your brand positioning.

Ensure the content is of high quality, consistent with your brand image, and capable of engaging the target audience.

c. Use Hootsuite for Content Distribution:

Upload your prepared content to Hootsuite.

Leverage Hootsuite's scheduling feature to set optimal publishing times based on the active hours of your target audience, ensuring that your content reaches a wider audience.

d. Implement Chatbots for Automated Interactions:

Integrate a chatbot on your social media pages or official website.

Configure automated responses to common queries, such as product

information, pricing, and purchasing methods.

When users interact with the chatbot, it can automatically address their

questions, enhancing user satisfaction and engagement rates.

e. Monitor and Analyze Data:

Utilize Hootsuite's data analytics capabilities to monitor the

effectiveness of your content, including metrics like views, likes, shares,

and more.

Based on data analysis results, adjust your content strategy, such as

modifying posting times or adding specific content types.

f. Optimize Customer Interactions:

Regularly review chatbot interaction records to identify new user needs

and issues.

Based on user feedback, optimize the chatbot's automated response

content to provide an improved user experience.

g. Generate Revenue:

Increase brand awareness and attract more target audiences by regularly publishing high-quality content.

Utilize the chatbot to enhance customer satisfaction and conversion rates, thereby boosting the sales of your products or services.

For individuals looking to promote their personal brand, combining AI tools with social media marketing strategies can effectively increase brand awareness and conversion rates. Through continuous optimization and engagement, you can build a loyal fan base and create long-term value for your brand.

AI Empowering Code Generation

Case: Individual Developer

a. Define Development Project:

Before starting coding, it's essential to clarify the type of project you want to develop, such as a web application, mobile app, desktop application, etc.

List out the main functional modules based on project requirements.

b. Initial Code Writing:

Begin writing initial code based on the functional modules.

During the coding process, you can utilize GitHub Copilot's code suggestion feature to help you write code faster.

c. Use GitHub Copilot for Automated Code Generation:

When encountering difficulties or uncertainties about how to implement a specific feature while writing code, you can enable GitHub Copilot's automatic code generation feature.

Input a description of the functionality you want to achieve, such as "Create a user login feature," and GitHub Copilot will generate corresponding code for you.

d. Code Review and Optimization:

After completing code writing, conduct a code review using DeepCode.

DeepCode automatically detects errors, vulnerabilities, and optimization suggestions within the code and provides you with repair solutions.

e. Testing and Deployment:

After code review and optimization, perform functionality testing to ensure code accuracy and stability.

Make necessary code modifications based on the test results.

Once testing is completed, deploy the project to a production environment.

f. Earning Revenue:

Publish your project on open-source platforms like GitHub to attract attention from other developers, gain Stars and Forks.

Set up donation links on project pages to encourage satisfied users to donate to your project.

Create a personal developer account on platforms like Freelancer and Upwork, showcase your project portfolio, and offer paid development services to clients.

In Summary

For individuals new to AI, by utilizing AI tools effectively, you can rapidly achieve revenue generation in various fields. This not only improves work efficiency but also opens up new income sources. The key is to choose the right tools, combine them with your expertise, and create a rational strategy that aligns with market demands.

The practice of restaurant chain companies using AI technology to select locations for entry and exit

In the restaurant industry, choosing the right location is one of the key factors determining success. Traditional site selection methods mainly rely on manual expertise and market research, but this approach is both time-consuming and less precise. With technological advancements, AI offers more accurate and efficient site selection solutions for foodservice businesses. Below, we will use the fictional "Foodie Paradise" restaurant enterprise as an example to explore how to integrate AI technology into site selection decisions.

data collection

Foodie Paradise began with comprehensive data collection:

- Demographic Data: This includes population density, age distribution, income levels, and more in the target area.

- Business Districts: Understanding the distribution of business centers, shopping malls, office areas, and the like within the target area.
- Competitive Landscape: Gathering information on the number, scale, and ratings of similar foodservice businesses within the target area.
- Transportation: Examining factors such as public transportation, subway lines, parking facilities, and their distribution.

Tool Selection

- DataRobot: This is an automated machine learning platform capable of automatically performing data preprocessing, feature engineering, model selection, and tuning. Its advantage lies in its ability to quickly train efficient models, significantly reducing model development time.
- Tableau: A powerful data visualization tool that transforms complex data into intuitive charts and maps, helping decision-makers better understand data.

Model Training:

Food Paradise chose two algorithms, Random Forest and XGBoost, for model training. Random Forest can effectively handle a large number of input variables and has excellent accuracy. XGBoost, on the other hand, is a boosting tree algorithm known for its outstanding performance in many data science competitions and is considered a "game-changer."

Intelligent Recommendations and Evaluation

After model training is completed, the evaluation of potential locations will be based on the following indicators:

- Sales Forecast: Estimated sales revenue for the new store in the next year.
- Average Customer Spend: Expected average expenditure per customer at the new store.
- Return on Investment (ROI): Anticipated return on investment for the new store.

Comparing Multiple Scenarios and Decision Support:

Assuming the AI system recommends two alternative options, Location A and Location B, for Food Paradise. The system will compare various indicators such as projected sales revenue, average customer spend, and ROI to assist decision-makers in clarifying the advantages and disadvantages of the two locations.

Detailed Report Generation

In the end, the AI system generated a comprehensive location assessment report for Food Paradise, including the following:

- Heatmaps: Displaying information such as foot traffic and consumer spending levels in the target area.
- Bar Charts: Comparing expected sales revenue, average customer spend, and more for different candidate locations.
- Pie Charts: Illustrating population demographics and consumption habits in the target area.

Conclusion

In the digital age, AI technology offers unprecedented possibilities for location decisions in the retail industry. Through data-driven approaches, businesses can not only assess the potential value of their store locations more accurately but also make decisions more quickly and efficiently. For retail and service-oriented enterprises, AI technology undoubtedly provides a competitive advantage and serves as a valuable success story for others in the retail sector to learn from. In this way, Food Paradise can not only evaluate the potential value of its store locations more precisely but also make decisions more swiftly and efficiently. This presents a new, more scientific approach to location selection for the foodservice industry.

CONCLUSION

Looking Ahead to the Future of AI Development and Creating More Business Value

Looking Ahead to the Future of AI Development and Creating More Business Value

What lies ahead for us in the future of AI, and how will it continue to create more business value for both enterprises and individuals?

Future Trends and Predictions for AI Technology

Greater Computing Power: With the development of technologies like quantum computing and neural network chips, future AI systems will possess more powerful computing capabilities, enabling them to handle more complex tasks and larger datasets.

Widespread Edge Computing: AI will no longer be limited to the cloud but will be deployed more extensively on edge devices, enabling real-time, low-latency intelligent applications.

Enhanced Autonomous Learning: Future AI systems will focus more on unsupervised learning and reinforcement learning, allowing them to autonomously learn and evolve without labeled data.

Stronger Interdisciplinary Integration: AI will undergo deep integration with multiple fields such as biology, neuroscience, and psychology, achieving higher levels of intelligence.

How AI Creates More Business Value for Enterprises and Individuals

Personalized Consumer Experience: Through deep learning and big data analysis, businesses can provide customized products and services to each consumer, achieving genuine one-on-one marketing.

More Efficient Production and Supply Chains: AI can assist businesses in achieving intelligent production scheduling, inventory management, and logistics optimization, significantly improving production efficiency and reducing costs.

Smarter Decision Support: With AI technology, businesses can achieve more precise market forecasts, risk assessments, and strategic planning, providing decision-makers with robust data support.

Wider Innovation Opportunities: AI offers endless innovation possibilities for individuals and businesses, ranging from content creation to product design and from service models to business models, potentially leading to disruptive transformations.

AI is not just a technological revolution but also a revolution in thinking. It is profoundly changing our lifestyles, workstyles, and ways of thinking. In the face of such a future full of boundless possibilities, we should embrace it with enthusiasm, courageously meet challenges, continuously learn and innovate, and work together with AI to create a brighter future.

Encouraging More Innovators to Embrace AI for Business Innovation

As AI technology matures, its applications in various industries are becoming increasingly widespread. For innovators, AI is not just a technical tool but also a mindset of innovation that can bring disruptive changes to business models, product design, service experiences, and more. Therefore, encouraging more innovators to adopt AI technology can not only enhance their competitiveness but also create more value for society as a whole.

Learning Resources and Entry Recommendations for AI Technology

Online Courses: Platforms like Coursera, Udacity, edX, and others offer a wide range of high-quality AI-related courses, covering various aspects from fundamental theory to practical applications.

Open Source Projects: Tools such as TensorFlow, PyTorch, Keras, and more are excellent deep learning frameworks with extensive documentation and community support.

Books: Titles like "Deep Learning" and "Machine Learning" are classic textbooks in the AI field, suitable for systematic learning.

Practice: When it comes to AI technology, the best way to learn is through practice. You can start with small projects such as image recognition, speech synthesis, recommendation systems, and gradually build up your experience.

How to Build an AI-Driven Innovation Team

Multidisciplinary Fusion: An AI team requires not only computer scientists and engineers but also data analysts, product managers, designers, and others to achieve interdisciplinary integration.

Continuous Learning: AI technology evolves rapidly, and team members need to maintain a continuous learning attitude, constantly keeping up with the latest technologies and applications.

Culture of Experimentation: Encourage team members to conduct various experiments without fearing failure. Learn from failures, iterate, and optimize continuously.

Close Integration with Business: AI technology needs to be closely integrated with actual business operations. Team members should have a deep understanding of business needs to ensure that technology can genuinely create value for the business.

AI technology offers limitless possibilities for innovators, but it also requires them to have a certain technical foundation and innovative thinking. Only by truly mastering AI technology can its maximum value be realized in business innovation.

APPENDIX

references

1. Goodfellow, I., Bengio, Y., & Courville, A. (2016). Deep Learning. MIT Press. [For foundational concepts and techniques in deep learning]

2. Vaswani, A., et al. (2017). Attention is all you need. Advances in Neural Information Processing Systems. [Original paper on the Transformer architecture and attention mechanism]

3. Radford, A., et al. (2019). Language models are unsupervised multitask learners. OpenAI Blog. [Introduction to the GPT-2 model]

4. Brown, T. B., et al. (2020). Language models are few-shot learners. Advances in Neural Information Processing Systems. [Research on the GPT-3 model]

5. Ruder, S. (2016). An overview of gradient descent optimization algorithms. arXiv preprint arXiv:1609.04747. [Overview of optimization algorithms used in training neural networks]

6. Brock, A., Donahue, J., & Simonyan, K. (2018). Large scale GAN training for high fidelity natural image synthesis. arXiv preprint arXiv:1809.11096. [Research on GANs, which are foundational for tools like DALL-E]

7. Kingma, D. P., & Ba, J. (2014). Adam: A method for stochastic optimization. arXiv preprint arXiv:1412.6980. [Introduction to the Adam optimization algorithm]

8. OpenAI. (2021). DALL·E: Creating Images from Text. OpenAI Blog. [Introduction to the DALL-E model]

9. Chollet, F. (2017). Deep Learning with Python. Manning Publications Co. [For foundational concepts in deep learning and practical applications]

10. Sutskever, I., Vinyals, O., & Le, Q. V. (2014). Sequence to sequence learning with neural networks. Advances in Neural Information Processing Systems. [Foundational work on sequence-to-sequence models, which are key for language translation tasks]

11. Hinton, G., Vinyals, O., & Dean, J. (2015). Distilling the knowledge in a neural network. arXiv preprint arXiv:1503.02531. [Research on model distillation, which is key for deploying large models in real-world applications]

Relevant industry reports and data sources

1. McKinsey & Company. (2019). Notes from the AI frontier: Applications and value of deep learning. [Provides insights into the applications and value of deep learning across various sectors]

2. Gartner. (2020). Magic Quadrant for Data Science and Machine Learning Platforms. [Evaluates the top platforms in the data science and machine learning industry]

3. Forrester Research. (2020). The Forrester New Wave™: AI-Driven Digital Advertising Platforms. [Analysis of AI-driven digital advertising platforms]

4. IDC. (2019). Worldwide Artificial Intelligence Systems Spending Guide. [Offers a quantitative assessment of the AI market and how it's expected to grow]

5. Statista. (2021). Artificial Intelligence - statistics & facts. [Provides a collection of statistics and facts about AI, including its commercial applications]

6. eMarketer. (2020). AI in Content Marketing. [Insights into how AI is transforming content marketing]

7. PwC. (2019). Sizing the prize: What's the real value of AI for your business and how can you capitalize? [Analysis of the economic potential of AI]

8. CB Insights. (2020). State of AI Report. [Annual report detailing the latest advancements and trends in AI]

9. World Economic Forum. (2018). Harnessing Artificial Intelligence for the Earth. [Report on how AI can be used to address environmental challenges]

10. Kaggle. (Various years). Datasets. [A platform that hosts a variety of datasets which can be used for AI and machine learning projects]

11. OpenAI. (Various publications). [Research papers, models, and datasets from one of the leading organizations in AI research]

12. Google AI. (Various publications). [Research papers and resources from Google's AI division]

13. MIT Technology Review. (Various years). AI Index Report. [Annual report that tracks, collates, distills, and visualizes data related to artificial intelligence]